STRONGER BECAUSE OF IT

A Woman's Journal on Her Spiritual Journey With Lupus

Laura Biernacki

CONTENTS

FOREWORD

Written by Alaina DaRin

Ever since I was a little girl, I always knew that I was being watched over by angels. I would go outside and feel the sunshine on my face and the gentle breeze blowing through my hair. I felt a complete sense of peace, and this to me, was what God was. As children, I believe we understand best what God is, and I truly felt in my heart that one day, I would help people see Him in everything.

When I first met my boyfriend, Matt, I never knew that I was a poet. As a child I had dreams of being a teacher and an artist, but as I got older, I grew further away from those dreams. Luckily, Matt brought out the best in me. His love helped me remember the messages that I always wanted to share with others. I began writing poetry as an outlet and I realized how self-soothing it was for me to write.

Matt and I both started sharing our poetry on Instagram, and the feedback and the support from the community was truly amazing. Matt began self-publishing his work in the form of small poetry books, and he inspired me to put together my own book. I remember one day, Matt received a message from a woman explaining how touched she was by his poetry and how much it helped her get through

her recent hospital visits. I felt so humbled that someone reached out to him and was comforted by his words.
I knew at that moment that the work we were doing was
not just for ourselves, but for others.

Without sharing our message, we would have never met
one of our now dearest friends, Laura. She taught me that
our words have the potential to change someone's life, and
she taught me that gratitude is a superpower. And to me,
she's the strongest superhero I know.
I hope this book will serve as an inspiration and a reminder
that we can turn our pain into purpose. Whether you have
experience with a chronic illness or someone close to you
has a chronic illness, or maybe you are just drawn to Laura's
story, I hope that Laura's words can provide comfort and
care during your most difficult times. No one should ever
have to feel alone, and I believe that together, we can truly
remind each other that we have always been on the path
towards selfless service.

PART ONE: THE BEGINNING

Symptoms and Diagnosis

I was diagnosed with Lupus when I was 28 years old. I was working as a hospice nurse in Detroit, Michigan at the time, but I started showing symptoms years before I was officially diagnosed. One of the very first symptoms I had was sensitivity to the sun. I had been dating a guy who had a speedboat at the time, and we had so much fun that we stayed out in the sun for hours. We would spend the entire day riding in his boat and swimming in the lake. But I started to notice that even though I was wearing sunscreen, I would still break out into a rash and get flu-like symptoms. I started to hate being out in the sun, which didn't help as I was young, single and in my twenties.

Another symptom I had discovered was sensitivity to chemicals. I used to be a blonde and loved getting highlights in my hair, but one day, my scalp reacted negatively to the hair dye and I started losing clumps of hair. This was really hard for me because I loved getting my hair done.

My main symptoms, though, started a couple of years later while I was working as a hospice nurse. I was experiencing fatigue that felt so deep to the bone. I had figured that I was just really tired from working at my new job. Anyone who has worked in the healthcare industry understands how hard the work can be. But the fatigue became so overwhelming that one time I had fallen asleep at the wheel; it had started to become a big problem and truly dangerous. No matter how much sleep I would get the night before, I would still fall asleep. I will never forget the time I woke up in a panic and realized that I had just driven through a red light on Gratiot Avenue during evening rush hour in Detroit. I must have had guardian angels watching over me because I never got into an accident.

I used to be so exhausted that I would go home and sleep for hours and still would never feel rested. Sometimes, I wouldn't be able to even fall asleep because I was so tired. The fatigue was different from anything I had experienced before. To make matters worse, I had also felt achy and experienced flu-like symptoms. What finally drove me to see a doctor was when I woke up one morning with a fever of 104 degrees, chills, body aches and joint pain that felt like broken bones. I also had the famous butterfly rash and pleurisy, which is common in Lupus patients. After months of medical tests, I was finally diagnosed with SLE, also known as Systemic Lupus Erythematosus.

SPIRITUALITY AND FAITH

I have always been a spiritual person and have always had a strong faith in God. I was raised Lutheran, but eventually converted to Catholicism. To this day, I still find great peace in attending mass and going into prayer. I have a deep faith in God and Jesus; I also read a lot of books on Buddhism and Eastern philosophy.

I have been blessed with psychic abilities, including having premonitions about people. Sometimes, I have been able to predict if someone was going to die through dreams and visions. I was able to see someone right before their death, even if I didn't know that they were sick. Both of my aunts were intuitive and one had mediumship abilities, so I had already been open to being an empath and having psychic abilities.

While I was waiting to find out if I had Lupus or not, I noticed my abilities strangely increasing. I started to feel when my patients had passed away, even before I was paged. There was a change in the atmosphere, almost like an electrical charge, and I would then get the call that one of my patients had died.

I also started having more spiritual dreams. One night, I prayed to God and asked Him if I had Lupus. That same night, I had a dream that there were two wolves staring at me and one of my spirit guides was standing there, too. I felt like I was being watched over. The next morning, I looked up the meaning of "wolf" and found out that "wolf" in Latin means "Lupus".

NEAR-DEATH EXPERIENCES

I have had many wonderful mystical experiences that have helped me with my faith in God. I have always had faith regardless, but these amazing experiences really sealed the deal. When I was in high school, I had a couple of visions where I had premonitions of peoples' deaths.

When I was first diagnosed with Lupus, I had kept feeling like I was fainting in my sleep and I would wake up really tired. I went to my doctor who wanted to check on my heart. He fitted me with a Holter monitor which I wore for a week. The monitor can detect if there are any abnormal heart rhythms and rates. Two of the nights I had a feeling of fainting. However during these times, I had incredible dreams which I now believe were near death experiences.

On the first night, I had felt myself faint, and then I found myself in a white bathtub in a white bathroom. I looked down at myself and saw that I was neither male nor female. I got up and started walking towards a door; I was about to open it when I realized that I would never wake up. I knew that if I walked through the door, I would die that night. I then heard music and singing that was not of this world, but somehow knew that it was angels telling me that it was not my time.

The next night, I had the same feeling of fainting in my sleep. This time, I was in a house looking out towards a corridor. I started walking towards the door towards the corridor, and once again, knew that once I walked out the door, I would not wake up, I would die in my sleep. I heard the otherworldly music and singing again that told me it was not my time.

When I went to my doctors for my results of the Holter monitor, he showed me that the nights that I had those near death experiences, my heart rate dropped to the twenties. He said that I could have died and if I started fainting during the day, I would need a pacemaker. However, it stopped happening, so I never needed a pacemaker.

What really confirmed my experiences was my father's death on February 15, 2020. I had put him in a hospice facility because he was actively dying. Those were his final wishes. He was comatose, so I went home to get some sleep. I woke up around 3 a.m. and tried falling back asleep, but I could not fall asleep, so I meditated instead. When I was deep in meditation, I saw my father walking with my mom down a similar corridor that I had started to go towards the time before. I woke up and knew that my father had died. In that same moment, his hospice nurse called me to say that he was passing. I really feel so blessed that I can experience death for myself and for other people. It gives me a profound sense of faith where I know that life continues after we die, just in a different form.

FAMILY LIFE AND CAREER

Unfortunately, my Lupus prevented me from maintaining my career as a hospice nurse. I was always calling in with a flare, so I needed to figure out what to do next. I had asked God if I was on the right path becoming a nurse. Later that night, I had a dream that I was in a forest surrounded by all of my family and friends. I told them goodbye and started walking down a path in the woods; it was so beautiful, I wanted to cry tears of joy. I looked over, and there was one of my guides, standing there looking at me. He nodded, then I turned into a wolf, running free into the night. I heard God's voice tell me, "this is your gift child". As it turns out, wolves are also symbols of healers, so I knew I had to somehow stay on my path as a healer.

In the midst of all this, I had been blessed with my boyfriend, John, who is now my husband. We were together for about 6 months before I was diagnosed. He was so supportive and I felt so grateful because sometimes people with chronic illnesses do not have such beautiful people in their lives.

John and I eventually got married and I became pregnant with a baby boy. Fortunately, my pregnancy went really well even though I was considered high risk because of having Lupus and being 36 years old. However, it didn't go without complications at birth since my son, Michael was breech. At the time, my physician was wise enough to know that I should not go into labor, and he also did not want to turn Michael. This was very prescient, because if I had tried to give birth, both Michael and I would have died. I had thankfully scheduled a C-section at

38 weeks, and Michael came out perfectly healthy, but the placenta had adhered to my uterus which caused me to almost bleed to death. My OBGYN had told me later on that this can happen to women with Lupus, but I was blessed to have such a skilled physician. He saved me and Michael's life.

MORE SYMPTOMS

Unfortunately, my Lupus started to get worse as time went on. I ended up being diagnosed with CNS Lupus, which started to affect my whole life. CNS Lupus is different from Lupus because there are more neurological symptoms such as extreme fatigue, joint pain, fevers, sun sensitivity, depression and anxiety.

Interestingly enough, my hallucinations were not scary, mostly entertaining, as they would consist of images from movies I watched. There was a time I was at the library standing next to a man, and when I looked over at him, he was headless like in the movie, *The Headless Horseman* with Johnny Depp. I had to do everything I could to stop myself from screaming, especially because I was in the library. After some time had passed, I got so used to the hallucinations that I didn't mind them, they were even fun sometimes. My friends were always so interested in what I was seeing and I did my best to keep my humor.

I had more serious symptoms with CNS Lupus, such as not knowing where I was, which was especially terrifying while I was driving. A few times I would be driving down the highway in Cleveland, Ohio and then I would suddenly not know if I was in Cleveland or Detroit, Michigan. I would also sometimes lose sense of time. One time I had been playing cards with my friends and I had suddenly forgotten a whole round of cards played. Another time, I found myself staring into the mirror, not remembering where I put my contact lenses. It took me a whole month to find them.

Those with Lupus understand how much it can affect their brain. There have been times when I would not be able to read people's facial expressions and would feel paranoid. One time, I had a friend say hello to me, but instead of seeing him happy, I saw his face as angry, almost evil looking. I thought he had a problem with me, but I then discovered later on that I was seeing people's facial expressions as distorted. I had also felt paranoid when I heard people laughing because I thought they were laughing at me. It was as if my whole perception of social cues were distorted.

I have also experienced severe mood swings and sudden fits of anger and debilitating depression. These symptoms sound like a mental illness, but my rheumatologist knew that it was the Lupus attacking my brain and its functions. At first he tried taking me off my medicine for Lupus. The medication at the time was raising my liver enzymes and damaging my liver, but I started having severe symptoms after I stopped taking it. Once he put me on high doses of Prednisone, my symptoms started to get better. However, it took a couple of years to find Rituxan, an infusion chemotherapy used for Leukemia; and Plaquenil, which finally alleviated most of my symptoms.

In the winter of 2017, I started throwing up blood. Then, I noticed blood in my stool and that I was losing weight rapidly. When I would try to eat, I would throw up; my reflux was getting worse. I started losing weight quickly because I had felt full after eating maybe a quarter cup of food. I also noticed that I had horrible constipation. I went from being slightly overweight for my height at 125 lbs, to 110 lbs within a matter of months. I ended up going to the emergency room because I had blood in my stool and abdominal pain.

My GI physician recommended an endoscopy. He

did not find anything abnormal like cancer, but I continued seeing him to figure out what was going on. I continued not being able to eat much because I would feel full. If I tried to force myself to eat, I would experience nausea, vomiting and stomach pain, so I continued losing weight.

At the time, the physician thought I had gastroparesis. We did a gastric emptying test which showed delay in my stomach emptying. My gastroenterologist, nurse practitioner and staff were so helpful; they suggested protein shakes and small meals. However, nothing worked, and I ended up dropping to 92 lbs.

My physician ended up putting in an NJ tube. It was awful because a radiologist had to thread a tube down my nose to my jejunum (located in the intestines) while I was awake. It was horrible, because I was always gagging. My husband described it as an almost medieval treatment.

The first time I tried tube feeding, I could not stop throwing up. I ended up being hospitalized because I was dying. Not only could I not eat, but I was also not getting any nutrition. My mesenteric artery collapsed and smashed my intestines so that the nutrients were not being absorbed. My physician told me that I had to either tube feed for 24 hours a day or risk organ failure. I walked around with a feeding tube coming out of my nose connected to a backpack with a pump and IV bag full of liquid nutrition. I refused to give up.

I was always big into working out and boxing with my friend and trainer, Joe. I was really weak at the time, but Joe knew how to work with me carefully. He helped me stay fit by letting me hit mitts. He would call out various punches and combinations. I think this was one of the ways I kept my positive attitude and humor about my situation, because there is nothing better than boxing to help you get rid of pent-up anger and frustration! As Joe liked to put it: "Best way to have fun without going to jail!" I still work with Joe boxing and lifting weights because exercise keeps me sane. I find sometimes that even if I'm having a flare, I still go to boxing. However, if my flare is really bad, I won't go.

I wore this badge of honor feeding tube for 2 months. I had a couple of issues with it though, like the time I had to go to the hospital because I was choking on my feeding tube and I thought I was dying. I love the movie *Alien*, so I felt like one of the characters being strangled by an alien popping out of my throat. Luckily, the tube stayed in and I went up to 105lbs. I know that doesn't sound like a lot, but I am a really small person, so that weight worked well for me.

The physician ended up pulling the tube, and I unfortunately lost a lot of weight. My physician then explained that I needed a more permanent solution, which meant a PEJ tube to be inserted surgically into my intestines. We were learning that I just could not maintain my weight without a feeding tube.

When I received my PEJ tube, I named it "Ripley" after the main character in *Alien*. I have found that humor is a wonderful way to cope with a bad situation. I still had to tube feed for 24 hours a day, so I wore a backpack again. Since I love to keep my humor, I found a sticker of the mouth from the movie *Alien* to decorate my backpack with.

The permanent feeding tube was much more comfortable than the tube that went down my throat, but it was far from perfect. When I first had my tube, my small intestines decided to freeze, meaning my intestines could not move normally to allow food to move through. Unfortunately, this caused a lot of excruciating pain and I was unable to tube feed.

I ended up in the emergency room where they found a mass in my lung. All I could think was *fudge*. The PET scan glowed, which meant I could have had a cancerous tumor, so they sent me off to surgery. I have an extremely high tolerance for pain, however, I was in pain not from the surgery, but from the actual chest tube. I was only 99 lbs at that time, which caused the chest tube to rub against my ribs. Thankfully, I had a fantastic surgeon with amazing nurse practitioners. They did an amazing job with pain control. When the nurse practitioner pulled out my chest tube, I felt no pain. That was an amazing feat! If you are in the medical field and have ever had a chest tube, you can understand my praises.

Luckily, my mass was benign. We believed it was fungus, because I had fungus all within my body. This was due to the immunosuppressant drugs I had to take for Lupus. I went to see an immunologist and it turned out that I had a suppressed immune system due to the medications. This is very common among people on these drugs. My immunologist put me on an IVIG that I did at home. They infused me with a pump, which was a miracle for me because my immune system was beginning to improve.

Meanwhile, I was still on tube feedings for over a year. I am so blessed to live in Cleveland where there is amazing medical care. The Cleveland Clinic and the University Hospital system both have amazing physicians. This is where my gastroenterologist and his nurse practitioner referred me to a popular physician at the Cleveland Clinic. This particular physician specializes in gastroparesis. My physician was not convinced that the problem was in my stomach, instead he thought it was more of a motility issue in my intestines. He felt that it was a problem with my Lupus or some other autoimmune disease. After all, if you have one autoimmune disease, it is much more likely to have another.

The gastroenterologist drew blood tests that I had never seen before. I also got to do the SmartPill test, which is a special camera that you swallow. Unfortunately, the smart pill only measures movement in your stomach and intestines; it did not take pictures. This saddened my friend and I because we weren't able to post it on Facebook or Instagram! We thought that it would be funny for our friends and family to see.

The doctor also had me do some very embarrassing but interesting tests to see if there was anything wrong with me anatomically. Did you know there is an actual X-ray that shows your skeleton using the toilet? It was actually kind of cool watching my skeleton going to the bathroom on an X-ray machine shaped as a potty. Again, one needs humor and a somewhat weird idea of what is interesting in order to cope with these things.

It turns out after all that was said and done, I have a rare autoimmune disease called Autoimmune Gastrointestinal Dysmotility Disorder. This is a neurological autoimmune disease that attacks the nerves that control the peristalsis (or movement) of the intestines. My intestines were not able to move very well; food would sit in my intestines rotting for days. People with normal intestines empty their food in 24-48 hours, but mine would take over 80 to possibly 100 plus hours to empty. Food would back up into my stomach and I would feel full, so I could not eat much without feeling full, feeling nauseated, throwing up and being in a lot of pain.

Luckily for me, my physician at the Cleveland Clinic knew about possible treatments that seemed to work. He recommended that I be put on high doses of IVIG to hopefully kickstart my peristalsis. Unfortunately, since I had been receiving various infusions already for Lupus, my veins were pretty much inaccessible. So I got another device put in my body called a "port". After all, Ripley needed a friend!

They were able to insert the port into my subclavian artery. This way, the nurse could just put the needle into my port instead of poking into my hard-to-access veins. Of course I had to name my port since my feeding tube was named Ripley. So my awesome friend and boxing trainer, Joe recommended I name it after Keanu Reeves, because it is close to my heart. Anyone who knows me knows how much I love Keanu Reeves.

WHY I WROTE THIS BOOK

When I was first diagnosed with Lupus, I was in my twenties. At the time, I had a patient with Lupus who was also in her twenties and died in hospice the same day I was diagnosed. I was scared, in denial, and not sure of what to do or where to turn. This was during the nineties when there were not many treatments or public knowledge about Lupus. The internet did not exist at the time where I could look for support, so my friend Sarah gave me a wonderful book by a friend of hers about Lupus and it really helped. Since the internet is now a place where people can readily receive knowledge and support, I want to help provide my perspectives and insights if it means I get to help someone else, even if it's just one person.

I was asked in October of 2019 to be a guest on my friends' Matt and Alaina's podcast to talk about how I have overcome a lot of suffering that has come from having a chronic illness. I have been told by a few people that I am an inspiration to them because I try to remain positive and strong despite everything that has happened to me. I was humbled by that description, because I have known so many warriors with much worse circumstances than me who I had felt were more inspirational than me. I have taken their compliment very seriously and have felt so grateful for their belief in me. They have inspired me to remain strong, humbled and positive.

The podcast episode that I recorded with my friends Matt and Alaina is called, "The Power to Overcome Our Suffering." Ultimately, it is about our calling to help others. Recording the episode had convinced me to write this book about my experience with Lupus.

I hope that through my writing, I can be of help for those struggling to find meaning in their diagnoses of any chronic illness and/or disease. This can be physical, mental or both. It really does not matter, because there is always trauma and suffering that goes along with these illnesses. This is not easy because no one wants to be sick, however, I had felt called to find some kind of meaning and purpose to my suffering; it was the best way for me to cope. It kept me from not curling up in a ball somewhere in the corner, although believe me, I have had plenty of those days too!

SUFFERING AND GRATITUDE

KRISTEN ARMSTRONG

Every morning I do my gratitude prayers, no matter how upset or distraught I am. I even use my hospital stays to wake myself up spiritually, with meditation, prayer, Qi-gong, and Tai Chi. I refuse to give up. I also watch the Star Wars movies and any movie with Keanu Reeves, including *John Wick*, which highlights our light and dark side, or in our reality, shadow work as an opportunity for growth.

I strongly believe in the power of gratitude. Even on days when you don't believe there is anything to be grateful for, there is always something. Today, you woke up alive, present, and with a roof over your head. These things may sound simple, but it can change your perspective often and quickly.

Some mornings I had woken up to the site around my feeding tube hurting, and then I had started thinking about all the chores I had to do. Then I looked down and saw that my dog had an accident and I needed to clean it up even though I was running late. I had also felt sick to my stomach that I wasn't sure if I could even use my feeding tube without getting sick.

Those are the mornings I ask, "what the hell should I be grateful for?" So I stop for a minute and I take a deep breath. I think of how lucky I am to be married to such a kind husband. I think of how blessed I am to have such a kind son with a big heart. I keep listing off blessings in my head while I'm getting ready for the day.

There are so many different ways to help yourself feel gratitude. Everyone is different in what works for them. I have listed a few things that have helped me:

- Keep a gratitude journal. It helps to write things down because it allows you to look back. Writing is a good way to put the idea in your brain!
- Keep a nice book with gratitude quotes by your bed, that way you can read them when you wake up in the morning and/or before you go to sleep.
- Every morning before you get out of bed, think of all the wonderful people in your life. You can list them in your mind. You can also think about the things that you have in your life, such as food to eat or a roof over your head.
- You can put post-it notes on your mirror of the things that you are grateful for.
- You can listen to meditations about gratitude on your phone or computer.
- If the weather permits, I have found a walk in nature really cheers me up. I feel so grateful for the beauty that surrounds me.

I have learned that this suffering has taught me that I need to live for God, to let go of attachments, and to live in silence sometimes. Letting go of parts of my ego has allowed me to be in service for others. It has also taught me to be more empathetic towards others, to be grounded and to know when to be silent. Our soul knows how to quiet the mind and to be in silence, allowing us to see the beauty in our suffering. It is through suffering that we can commune with God, similarly to us taking a walk in nature or doing spiritual treatments such as Reiki.

Emotionally, my faith is what has helped me understand why I am going through all of this, and it allows me to try to stay positive and strong. I don't look to suppress my emotions so that people see me as happy all the time. This illness has brought me to my knees many times and has truly humbled me. Without my chronic illness, I don't think I would be the same person I am today.

"Have compassion for everything that you're feeling, it takes a tender touch to relieve you of your suffering."

MATT BUONOCORE

PART TWO: MY JOURNAL

April 18, 2018

Here I am, rocking the NJ tube! The NJ tube is a thin tube that goes down the nose and into the intestines. It is then hooked to a pump with an IV bag that is filled with liquid food. This is the only way at this point that I am able to eat, get my nutritional needs and gain some weight. Unfortunately, I am only 92 lbs from being 120 lbs. But, I am so grateful for my family and friends and the support they give. The support and prayers have helped me so much because getting the NJ tube went so much better than I thought it would!

LAURA BIERNACKI

JUNE 5, 2018

Feeding tube free and feeling much better! No more feeling like Sigourny Weaver from *Alien*! I am now weighing in at 105 lbs and hoping to maintain this weight.

NOVEMBER 21, 2018

I am receiving a new infusion called IGA. This will hopefully help boost my immune system. As most Lupus warriors understand, the medications we receive that help control Lupus will also affect our immune system from working to its highest potential. Hopefully, this will help before I get my Rituxan infusion next month. Also, not only did I receive the infusion, but I did end up getting a more permanent feeding tube, which is the yellow tube shown in this picture.

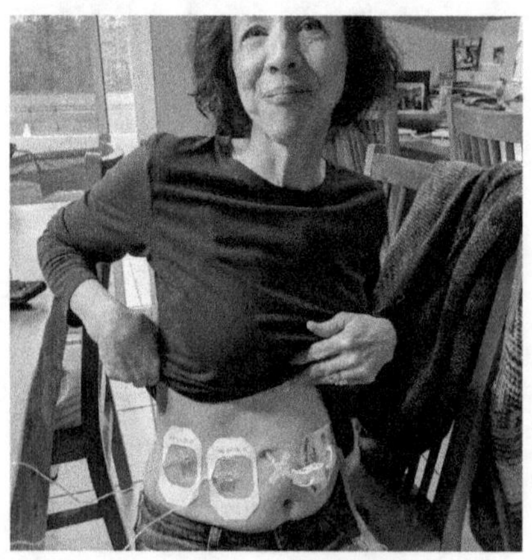

DECEMBER 7, 2018

I am so thankful for all of the wonderful nurses and staff at the Seidman Cancer Center in Cleveland, Ohio. I am getting my Rituxan infusions which is helping me so much. I am also so grateful to my wonderful rheumatologist, Dr. Riaz Ahmad and his awesome staff. He and my previous rheumatologist, Dr. Richard Stein, who is now retired, helped me by prescribing this infusion to control and stop the symptoms of the CNS Lupus from taking over my life.

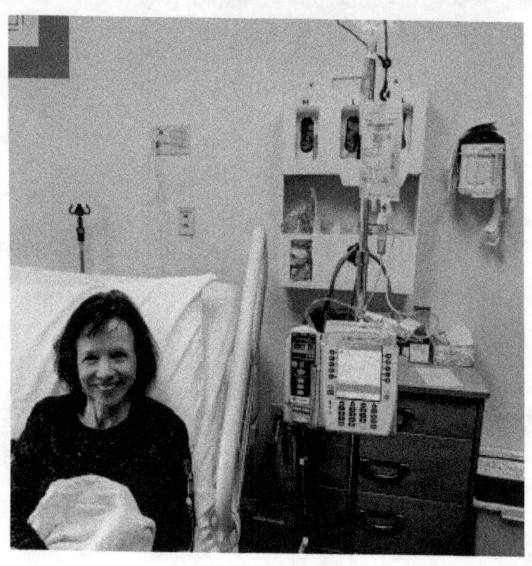

JANUARY 10, 2019

AUTHOR UNKNOWN

I love this quote. I have had a rough summer due to Lupus and gastroparesis. I almost had organ failure at one point. I also had a cancer scare from a mass in my lung. Luckily, it was benign.

I have always tried to stay strong, positive and have total faith in God. After this summer, I started feeling a need to do more spiritually. I have gone back to Tai Chi, Reiki, meditation, prayer and trying to spread more love and good ju-ju. I am definitely feeling better mentally, physically and spiritually.

FEBRUARY 4, 2019

Back in the hospital for a possible gastroparesis Lupus flare. Luckily, the pain medicine is starting to work. However, I hate coming to the hospital for pain, because I do not like pain medicine. It makes me feel nauseated and it also gives me a bad headache.

Usually, I treat my pain through various ways such as Reiki, Qigong and meditation. I also have an amazing friend, Jennifer who is a massage therapist. She is also an autoimmune chronic illness warrior, so she understands me. I have found that by getting a massage from her really helps with my pain physically, mentally and spiritually. However, there are times I still have to go to the hospital for pain control. But I have found that by doing these practices, I am able to avoid the hospital a lot more!

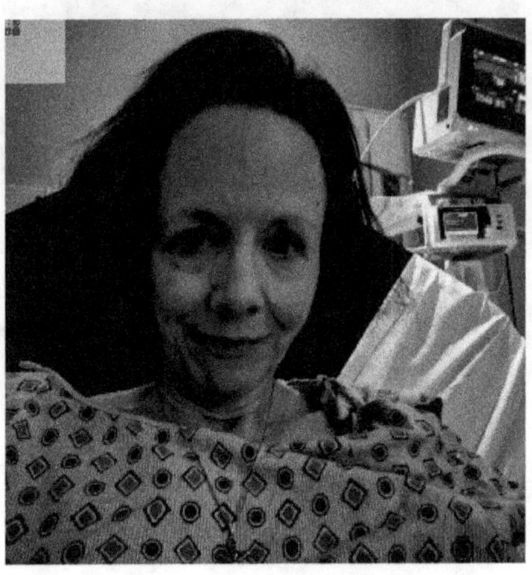

FEBRUARY 16, 2019

Yay! I have discovered something new and delicious! I have been drinking celery juice with some other veggies and fruit for the past month. I am hoping it will help with my Lupus and gastroparesis. Thank you so much to my killer boxing and fitness trainer, Joe Mazzone for the good recommendation and my friend, Julie Stavoli. Sending my love to everyone!

MAY 3, 2019

Here I am wearing green for Gastroparesis Awareness Day!

MAY 10, 2019

I am wearing purple along with my wonderful boxing and fitness trainer, Joe Mazzone for Lupus Awareness Day. I have had Lupus for over 20 years. My awesome friend and trainer has really helped me keep fit mentally and physically. He is a trainer who really understands when I can go strong, and when I am having a flare and need to take it easy.

JUNE 6, 2019

Yay! I am smiling because my insurance company has finally approved Rituxan, a drug that helps my brain which has been affected by Lupus. I have been receiving this infusion for a couple of years at the Westlake Ohio Seidman Cancer Center. It is the only medicine that has truly worked for me and I am so thankful!

I am also grateful for all of the nurses and staff here. It has been a tough year and a half due to my Lupus and gastroparesis, but it has helped me wake up spiritually. I have also found that I need to help others when I have the energy, so I have decided that I am going to get recertified as a Reiki practitioner!

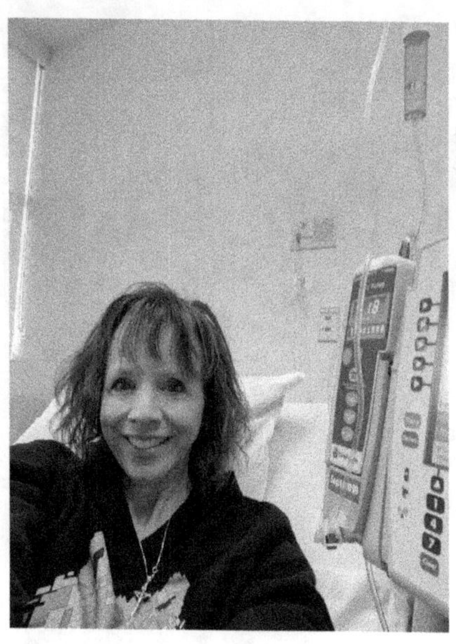

SEPTEMBER 7, 2019

Thank you so much to everyone who came out to the annual Cleveland Ohio Lupus Walk. It meant so much to me! I want everyone to know how truly grateful I am for the love and support. I love you guys and feel so blessed to have you all in my life. This is such an important cause to raise money for because so many are affected by this disease. I also want to thank the friends and family members who were unable to make it to the walk but still supported me. I am so grateful for your love and support.

*Side note: My friend Toni is not in this group picture. She is the woman in the background talking to a friend of hers from work!

OCTOBER 8, 2019

Hi everyone! I usually try to post happy stuff, but today, I am sad. Unfortunately, we had to put down our old and beloved dog, Jasper today. It was tough, but he was in a lot of pain and having a hard time breathing. So I know we did the right thing.

Now I know he is having a wonderful time in Heaven playing with Livia, Jae, Octo, Bud and all of his other friends. I asked my Aunt Deanne and Uncle Chet up in Heaven to help Jasper. They were true animal lovers. I know he is happier and free from all of his pain and suffering. Thank you for listening, everyone. Love you all.

NOVEMBER 4, 2019

I have found this beautiful park where I live in Cleveland, Ohio. I love being in nature because it helps me feel closer to God. I love to come here and ground myself, meditate and practice my Qigong and Tai Chi. When I do these beautiful practices, I find that I am a better Reiki practitioner, mom, friend and hopefully someone who spreads love and light to everyone. I find it so important to practice self care. How do you practice self care?

NOVEMBER 6, 2019

I want to thank my awesome boxing and fitness trainer, Joe Mazzone. I have worked with him for almost 8 years! He really understands my Lupus and autoimmune disease of the stomach and intestines. He knows when he can push me and when to take it easy. He also knows that when I cancel, it's because I am flaring up, and not because I am lazy!

Many times people with autoimmune diseases don't look sick, so sometimes we are mistaken for being lazy. I know it sounds ridiculous, but those thoughts from others exist. However, I am blessed with such wonderful people in my life who truly understand.

I love boxing because it is such a great stress reliever. I have had to learn that I can't always box due to flares, so I am really grateful on the days that I can exercise. I love to do Tai Chi, Qigong and meditation. I am sending everyone lots of love and light!

DECEMBER 19, 2019

I am now on week 14 for my infusion for my autoimmune gastrointestinal dysmotility disorder. With Lupus, it is really common to have other autoimmune diseases. This one is a rare disorder that affects my nervous system, and it is controlling the peristalsis of my intestines. Since I don't have any motility in my intestines, I get full from food very quickly. Therefore, I haven't been able to maintain my nutrition or weight.

I was referred to a wonderful specialist, Dr. Cline at the Cleveland Clinic by my amazing gastroenterologist, Dr. Newton, who wanted to see if there was a way to get me off of my tube feedings. So, Dr. Cline put me on infusions and they are working! I am still on continuous tube feedings, but I am now able to start eating again. It has been a year and a half since I have been able to eat a small meal, so I am really excited.

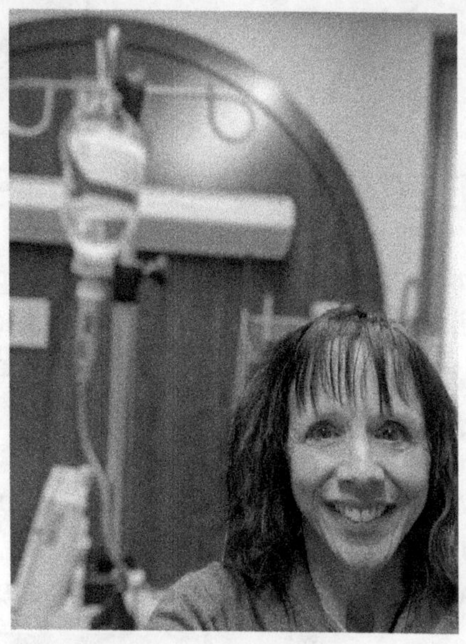

DECEMBER 31, 2019

I want to wish everyone a very Happy New Year! I am so grateful and thankful for all of you and for your love and support. It means so much to me. I am really happy here because I had a beautiful dinner with my family for New Year's Eve. I was able to eat some salmon and rice with a couple bites of apple crisp! It felt so awesome to eat! I am so grateful. Thank you so much and I hope that everyone has a blessed and beautiful 2020. Love you guys.

JANUARY 6, 2020

Hi everyone! I love Keanu Reeves. I love him because he is so strong, not just physically, but also emotionally. He truly is a warrior. When I was at my sickest and unable to do much, I would watch his movies like *John Wick*. He inspired me to keep going. Both Keanu Reeves (in real life) and his character, John Wick kept getting knocked down but never gave up. I feel a lot of gratitude and love for Keanu Reeves. Who inspires you?

JANUARY 7, 2020

I keep seeing this beautiful blue heron at our local park. I have always found nature healing. I read that the blue heron is a symbol of learning to stand on your own two feet and following your own path. It is important to know what works best for you and not worry so much about following others. If we listen closely to our hearts, we can feel what God wants us to do. This is not always easy, but it is so important. I hope everyone has a beautiful day. Sending you all love and light!

JANUARY 8, 2020

Hi everyone! I love this quote from my friends, Matt and Alaina from The Spiritual Spruce. It is so easy to get wrapped up in everyday life that we forget why we are really here. Ultimately, this life is about learning, growing, and spreading the message of love.

We have a mission in life to help others. I don't mean that we have to give up everything and become saints, because believe me, I am far from being a saint! Smiling at someone or saying something positive are the little things that really help.

I love this post because it is also a reminder that we are not alone. Whether we believe in God or a divine being, it doesn't matter. Jesus was amazing, and it is beautiful to aspire to be like him because He was true, unconditional love. How beautiful. I hope everyone has a wonderful day!

"Walk like Christ. Never alone, with great faith, and in mission. Your message is love."

THE SPIRITUAL SPRUCE

JANUARY 20, 2020

I was recently at Pokemon State Park in Indiana with my husband and friends. It was a beautiful experience! I found that being in nature and being in the moment with the ones you love, surrounded by God's love and light, is magical and mystical. We all need to recharge and take a break to get back to our heart and soul.

I am so grateful for this beautiful weekend with such beautiful people and surroundings. I am also blessed to be able to share this wonderful experience with all of my friends on social media.

JANUARY 25, 2019

Hi everyone! I found this quote on Facebook from "Divine Nectar". My friend, Dana Quarnstrom posted it first. I find that it really appeals to me and many people. Grief, and all that comes with it, is a part of life. Pain, emotional and spiritual, is a part of life, yet, so many of us do not want other people to see us in pain or feeling sad, angry or any other emotion that doesn't look happy. However, it is so important to find ways to express our grief, whether it is through exercise, writing, meditation, or beating up your heavy bag! I believe that you just need to find whatever works for you. Just make sure you find ways to let it out so it doesn't hurt you inside! Sending you all so much love.

JANUARY 26, 2020

I love Bruce Lee, he was an amazing person! This quote by him is so inspiring. We all go through our ups and downs. We must process and deal with our emotions to heal, and sometimes the emotional, spiritual and physical pain can be so overwhelming that we feel like giving up. This is completely normal and understandable.

This quote has helped me to keep going, no matter how bad I'm feeling. It makes me realize that I am a fighter! I wanted to post this in hopes that it will inspire others to keep fighting, even during difficult times.

"Even when you're down, look up. Look at what you must defeat and then get up and fight."

BRUCE LEE

FEBRUARY 3, 2020

I love being a Reiki practitioner because God gave me this beautiful gift as a channel to help others. I feel strongly that we are all born with beautiful gifts from God that need to be used in our lifetime. However, to be effective in using our spiritual gifts, whatever they may be, we need to love ourselves first. We have to go it alone and trust God that we can do this by ourselves.

It is wonderful to have a partner in life, but ultimately no one else can live our lives for us. We have to rely on ourselves to be happy and confident in ourselves and our abilities. This beautiful knowledge of being happy and confident without relying on anyone else is a great feeling of freedom.

FEBRUARY 6, 2020

Hi everyone! I got my port surgically inserted yesterday, so they no longer have to use my veins! I have been getting infusions for a long time now (about 6 years) and my veins have been increasingly inaccessible. But now I have a port and it's awesome! My infusion is running now, and I am a happy camper. I named my feeding tube "Ripley" after the main character in *Alien*, since it is jutting out of my intestines like an alien. And I named my port after Keanu Reeves because it is close to my heart. You guys all know how much I love Keanu Reeves! I hope he doesn't mind, ha! Sending you guys so much love and light.

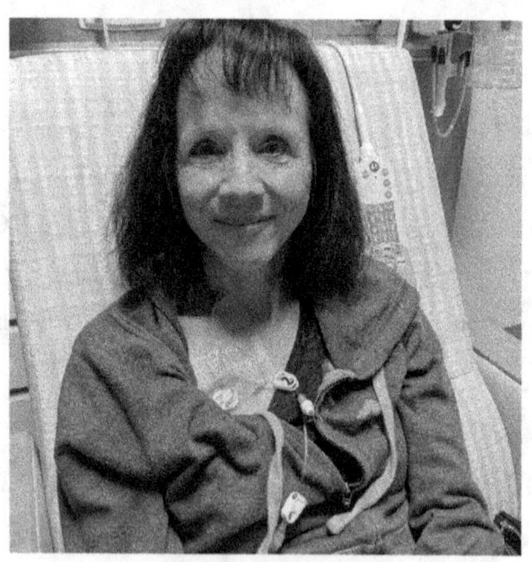

FEBRUARY 27, 2020

Hi everyone! I am so grateful for all of you. I feel so blessed to have such wonderful friends in my life that are so supportive. I appreciate everyone on social media and my friends and family that I have known for many years. I lost my father two weeks ago and unfortunately, with all of the stress from my autoimmune diseases, I went into full flare. Since I have such a beautiful support system in my life, I was able to bounce back rather quickly. I just wanted to say thank you to everyone. Sending you guys lots of love and light.

"Grateful for the big things,
grateful for the little things,
grateful for everything."

ALAINA DARIN

FEBRUARY 29, 2020

I found this beautiful quote by Midrash. It reminds me of how important it is to look at everything that we have been through that has caused us pain as an opportunity to grow. This is really hard to do when you are going through something difficult, but I have noticed that I would not be the same person I am today if I hadn't gone through tough times. If I hadn't fallen into darkness, I would not have seen the beautiful light from God and the Divine.

"Had I not fallen, I would not have arisen. Had I not been subject to darkness, I could not have seen the light."

MIDRASH

MARCH 10, 2020

Hi everyone! This quote is perfect because like everyone else, I sometimes get super busy and forget to think about all of the things that I am grateful for in the morning. It is easy to only think about the stuff that needs to be accomplished that day, like running errands, getting to work on time, helping the kids with their homework, etc. I find that when I wake up and think about everything that I am grateful for, my day is so much better and my mood is brighter. I am just thankful to be alive! Sending you guys so much love and light.

"We forget that waking up each day is the first thing we should be grateful for."

AUTHOR UNKNOWN

MARCH 13, 2020

Hi everyone! I love this quote by Mandy Hale. It is so easy to get stuck in a rut or a situation that is comfortable even though it causes you pain. It is hard to let go, but there is a lesson in this, too! Not everyone or everything is meant to stay in your life; sometimes they are there to teach you something. When things get hard, it feels so much better to free yourself. After a while, you will see the lessons and work towards growth.

"Growth is painful. Change is painful. But nothing is as painful as staying stuck somewhere you don't belong."

MANDY HALE

MARCH 15, 2020

Hi everyone! I hope you guys are surviving this zombie apocalypse. I love this quote from *Dune* by Frank Herbert. He is basically saying that fear can paralyze us. It is the "little-death" that can mess with our heart and thoughts. It will cause us to withdraw, instead of acting like the beautiful souls that we truly are.

I understand right now why people are scared. I have Lupus, asthma, and autoimmune gastrointestinal dysmotility who is on a lot of immunosuppressant drugs. I am immunocompromised like many others with various illnesses. I have been like this for at least 10 years. I am being careful, but I am also trying to stay calm, grounded and positive. I am trying to enjoy walks in the park and carve out extra time for Qigong, meditation and Reiki distance healing for anyone who needs it.

This has been my world for many years like so many others I know. So please, everyone, be careful and use your common sense. Try not to panic as best you can! Use this time for growth. Sending you lots of love and light.

LAURA BIERNACKI

"I must not fear. Fear is the mind-killer. Fear is the little-death that brings total obliteration. I will face my fear. I will permit it to pass over me and through me. And when it has gone past I will turn the inner eye to see its path. Where the fear has gone there will be nothing. Only I will remain."

DUNE, FRANK HERBERT

MARCH 25, 2020

Hi everyone! I hope you guys are hanging in there. I know that this is a difficult time with having to quarantine and social distance. It is hard for me because I am someone who loves to hug everyone. Yikes!

However, I love this quote from Albert Einstein. During all this time being stuck at home, I have really used this opportunity for spiritual growth and for following the path that I believe God wants me to follow. I am a Reiki practitioner and I have upped my long-distance Reiki sessions for many people who need the extra support.

I am considered a high-risk person because I have Lupus, autoimmune gastrointestinal dysmotility disorder and asthma. I am also immunocompromised due to the medications I take, such as chemotherapy. I point this out because I don't want to focus on the fear but on the positive. We all have beautiful gifts that we can send out to others from home, like poetry and humor on social media. We can all use this time to grow spiritually, so when this is over, we are at a beautiful place. Sending you guys so much love and hugs!

"In the middle of
difficulty lies
opportunity."
ALBERT EINSTEIN

APRIL 4, 2020

Hi everyone! I hope everyone is staying safe and healthy. I found this beautiful quote by Naguib Mahfouz. I love this, because right now things are scary and lonely for many of us. But the beauty of this time is how we use our time during social distancing. I have noticed so many wonderful posts about people using this time to meditate, walk in nature, create beautiful art and spread kindness. This is a perfect time to grow spiritually and to send love out into the world. Personally, I love doing my part by offering long-distance Reiki. Please let me know if you want a session for free! Sending you guys lots of love and light.

"Fear does not prevent death. It prevents life."

NAGUIB MAHFOUZ

APRIL 14, 2020

Hi guys! I hope everyone is doing well with all of the crazy things that are happening in this world. I found this amazing quote by Anthon St. Maarten about being an empath. I am an empath, which is a wonderful gift, especially being a Reiki practitioner. This gift helps me understand my clients. But the main problem I encounter is absorbing other people's energy, good or bad.

I have worked hard to learn how to manage this in a positive way and let go. However, with all of the anxiety and stress in the world right now, I noticed that I am having a lot of nightmares and negative energy around me. I think there are many of you out there that experience the same thing.

So, I am ramping up my coping mechanisms. I am waking up early so I can say my gratitudes, pray and meditate. I have also found that I need to add an extra 10-15 minutes of boxing. I have been focusing a lot on my Qigong and grounding as well. I have found that by doing energy work and protecting my energy, I am coping much better. How do you guys cope with the stress in the world right now? Sending you guys lots of love and light.

"Empaths did not come
into this world to be
victims, we came to be
warriors. Be brave. Stay
strong. We need all
hands on deck."

ANTHON ST. MAARTEN

APRIL 18, 2020

Hi everyone! I hope you guys are staying safe and healthy. I am getting bundled up to go on a hike on this beautiful trail in Cleveland, Ohio. It is 38 degrees out, brr!

Last night, I had another nightmare about having to sage my bedroom due to negative energy. It was scary; I woke up with anxiety. However, in my dream, my mom was there to help me and protect me. She crossed over in 2000; that was the beautiful part. I realized that I need to embrace my gifts as an empath and Reiki practitioner instead of fearing it.

We all have these wonderful gifts from God. I know they can be overwhelming, especially during times like these when there is a lot of fear in the world, but we are not alone. God would never give us gifts that we couldn't handle. We are all here to use our gifts to help each other and to love each other. We are here to heal ourselves; when we do, we heal others and the world.

I hope everyone is embracing their gifts and sending out their love and light. Take care!

APRIL 19, 2020

I found this quote by Jake Woodard and fell in love with the message. This is such a beautiful way of saying what I really have been trying to express in my last couple of posts. We are all going through tough times right now, but we can choose either to let it spiral us into experiencing anxiety and negativity, or we can use that pain and turn it into something good, such as spiritual growth. When we do that, our own garden grows into something beautiful. We can then spread the beauty to others and we can send our love and light!

"Imagine your mind like a garden and your thoughts are the seeds. You get to choose what seeds you plant in it. You can plant seeds of positivity, love, and abundance. Or you can plant seeds of negativity, fear, and lack. You can also spend time trying to take care of everyone else's garden. Or you can work on making yours beautiful and attract other beautiful people to your garden."

JAKE WOODARD

APRIL 24, 2020

Hi everyone! I hope you guys are doing well with this quarantine. I know it can be tough, but I thought I would share this beautiful quote. I have mentioned various ways that have helped me deal with anxiety, which I pray helps others. One of my favorite ways is to think about what I am grateful for. It definitely brings my vibration up. I know so many of you would agree too.

I am grateful for my family, my friends, my home and my health. I am grateful for my wonderful physicians and the healthcare workers that are keeping me strong and able to handle my Lupus. I am also so grateful for all of those front lines workers who are keeping us going during this quarantine. Sending you guys so much love and light!

"Gratitude helps you fall in love with the life you already have."

AUTHOR UNKNOWN

MAY 23, 2020

Hi everyone! I hope you guys are doing well. I found this gem on Pinterest. It is a quote by Michael P. Watson. I think especially at this time, we need some humor. But this quote is also very true. It is so beautiful to help each other and raise each other up.

We need to realize how we are actually connected; that we are more alike than different. That when we raise each other up and help each other out, we then raise the vibration of the planet. We can help in big ways, like helping all of the beautiful front liners. Or we can help in little ways with a smile, a word of encouragement or a compliment. That really makes a difference. As St. Thérèse de Lisieux said, "Miss no single opportunity of making some small sacrifice, here by a smiling look, there by a kindly word; always doing the smallest right and doing it all for love." Sending everyone lots of love and light!

"Strong people don't put
others down. They lift
them up."
MICHAEL P. WATSON

JUNE 13, 2020

Hi everyone! I have found myself doing more spiritual work early in the morning to center and ground myself before the day begins. I found this beautiful and peaceful spot in our local park while hiking that is quiet and private. Here, I can do my Qigong and meditation in nature where the energy is so positive and I feel closest to God. It is a wonderful way to start the day. How do you guys like to start your day? Sending you all lots of love and light!

JUNE 22, 2020

I found this wonderful quote from redemptionstouch.com. I am having a tough time with my neurological Lupus lately. Unfortunately, my insurance changed and I had to change infusion companies. Although it will be a blessing to have my Rituxan infusions at home, it caused a couple weeks delay in getting my Rituxan infusion. I am finally getting it tomorrow. However, my Lupus is causing all sorts of yucky neurological symptoms, including anxiety, dizziness, confusion, hallucinations, mood swings, tremors and feeling really cold all the time. This is because the Lupus is attacking my brain and nervous system. Luckily, I know this is temporary. Please know that I am not complaining, because I know it could definitely be worse. I am just really not feeling myself lately, so I am not doing much on social media. I am taking a break until I can get back to my goofy self! I love you guys so much.

"Leave room for God to
send you on detours because
the blessings may come on
the paths that you didn't
expect to take."

WWW.REDEMPTIONSTOUCH.COM

JUNE 26, 2020

Hi everyone! I want to thank all of you for the out-pouring of love, prayers and support during this difficult time with my Lupus. It really helped. I am feeling so much better now that I got my Rituxan infusion, plus all of your positive energy. I am so grateful for all of you. I love you guys so much. I hope everyone is doing wonderful. I am sending you lots of love and light.

JULY 12, 2020

I found a new trail this morning! I am so grateful for this beautiful day in Cleveland. My infusions are working beautifully and I am able to eat and enjoy. I am so blessed and grateful for my family, friends and the amazing medical people here. Thank you for all your love.

AUGUST 10, 2020

Hi everyone! I hope you guys are doing well. This is such an amazing quote by Millie Mestril. I am so grateful to everyone I know in my life. I believe that because of you, I am doing so much better than expected with my autoimmune diseases. I wanted you guys to know that I am starting a Facebook group for those who are diagnosed with a chronic and/or terminal illness. I think it is so important to support each other. Please let me know if you or someone you know is interested in joining! Sending you guys lots of love and light.

"I woke today with gratitude for those who share me in their lives. I am thankful for those who are part of my journey."

MILLIE MESTRIL

AUGUST 11, 2020

I love this quote by Shayne McClendon. I have found that no matter how anxious I feel or how sick I feel, this works. Because when I breathe, I stop my mind from over-thinking. This allows me to center myself in my heart and find better ways of coping.

> "I will breathe. I will think of solutions, I will not let my worry control me. I will not let my stress level break me. I will simply breathe. And it will be okay. Because I don't quit."
>
> SHAYNE MCCLENDON

AUGUST 12, 2020

Hi everyone! I have always found that gratitude is one of the best ways to help me stay in a positive mindset. Even if I wake up crabby, I find that having gratitude helps me get back to joy. I wanted to express my gratitude to my awesome nurse, Karen from Accredo. She comes over to my house every other week to give me my infusions for my autoimmune gastrointestinal dysmotility. I am so grateful for her positive energy and compassion. She is amazing! Plus, after almost two years of having to rely on tube feeding, I am able to eat again! This is truly something to be grateful for. What are you grateful for?

AUGUST 14, 2020

Hi everyone! I just want to remind everyone that I think it is so important to help each other out in a positive way, especially now when things are tough. I want to share my gratitude for finding Matt and Alaina on Instagram. When I was in the hospital around 2018, I wanted to read something positive on social media. That is when I met Matt. I started reading his poetry, which I found very spiritually uplifting. After connecting with him, I met his lovely girlfriend, Alaina. She also writes very beautiful and soulful poetry. These two have really helped me get through some tough times. They are now a part of my life as wonderful friends and guides. Sending you all lots of good vibes.

"We are the way-showers that will guide the world into the frequency of love. We have come for this mission, and we have only begun."

MATT BUONOCORE

AUGUST 16, 2020

Hi everyone! I hope you are all doing well. I have been feeling really anxious lately and I couldn't understand why. My father passed away in February of this year and I haven't had any time to grieve. But today, I lost it. I cried and cried. I guess as much as I try to stay positive for everyone, I also have my days. It is completely normal to cry. We need to. My father's death was eventually a blessing because he was so sick and suffering a lot. I was even blessed with a vision of him leaving with my mom. I have been blessed with many mystical experiences surrounding God and death; I have had great faith. I still miss my dad and mom, but I know that they are both doing awesome. Sending you guys so much love and light.

"Luminous beings are we, not this crude matter."

YODA, STAR WARS: EPISODE V - THE EMPIRE STRIKES BACK

AUGUST 18, 2020

I feel the most calm in my life, no matter what is going on, when I ground myself through Qigong and by staying present. But believe me, this is easier said than done. However, when we stay present, we cannot worry about the future or beat ourselves up over the past. What do you do to stay present and calm in the midst of a storm? Sending you all lots of love and light!

"Peace - It does not mean to be in a place where there is no noise, trouble or hard work. It means to be in the midst of those things and still be calm in your heart."

AUTHOR UNKNOWN

AUGUST 22, 2020

Hi everyone! I love this quote. I think it is the whole foundation on how I have outlived what my doctors thought would happen. I have tried my best to use all of my mental, physical and spiritual pain as ways to grow closer to God. I am not saying that I didn't have really bad days, because I did. But I have always tried. I also know that pain is miserable and this is nothing that I would wish on anyone. This is just my way of dealing with my situation in a way that works best for me. How do you deal with your pain?

"We can use the pain and turn it into spiritual growth."

AUTHOR UNKNOWN

SEPTEMBER 1, 2020

Hi everyone! I hope you all are doing well. I wanted to share this unflattering picture of me and George, "The Goiter", ha! I have been struggling the past few weeks of not feeling one hundred percent, but trying hard to keep going.

I have also been diagnosed with Lupus attacking my autonomic nervous system, which is called POTS. But honestly, I am grateful because everything is autoimmune and I already know that monster! Plus, I am so blessed to have such a wonderful medical community surrounding me in Cleveland.

I am so grateful for all my friends and family. I have found that these times of suffering are the most profound for spiritual growth. Not that I want to suffer, but I really try hard to find the positive. I do my best to use these times to find purpose, especially spiritually. How do you guys deal with your suffering? Sending everyone lots of love and light.

SEPTEMBER 14, 2020

Lord, make me an instrument of your peace:
where there is hatred, let me sow love;
where there is injury, pardon;
where there is doubt, faith;
where there is despair, hope;
where there is darkness, light;
where there is sadness, joy.

ST. FRANCIS OF ASISI

I heard this prayer from St. Francis of Asisi and discussed it in mass yesterday, along with the need to forgive and how forgiveness helps bring peace to both people. I also remember a conversation I had with a friend on Friday about a person that was so mean to me and it was hard to let go of my anger towards them. But my friend reminded me how much trauma this person had suffered in life.

I realized that this person probably was taking their anger and insecurities out on me. I suddenly felt sadness and compassion for the other person. I realized that in order for me to move on and let go of my anger, I needed to forgive.

This is not easy, but necessary. I do not want to leave this world with a heavy or angry heart. What do you do when you are angry at someone else and can't seem to let it go? How do you find peace?

SEPTEMBER 25, 2020

I am so excited because I am starting a new spiritual journey in October. I am becoming a Death Doula and classes start in October! A Death Doula is similar to a Birth Doula, but instead of helping with the birth process, I will be helping people in their death process. I am really happy because I will be able to use my hospice nursing experience, counseling, and Reiki experience. Plus, I have a lot of experience in my own life with family and friends dying. How are you guys doing in your spiritual journey?

OCTOBER 8, 2020

"If you knew who walked beside you at all times, on the path that you have chosen, you could never experience fear or doubt again."

WAYNE DYER

I wanted to share this beautiful quote with everyone because it holds so much truth. If you knew who walked beside you at all times on the path that you have chosen, you would never experience fear or doubt again. Beautiful and so true.

OCTOBER 14, 2020

I love this beautiful prayer I found. I always try to say something like this every day. I am especially reminded of my gratitude when I am able to hike and surround myself in nature. Being in nature, I feel one with God. Where do you find your happiness and joy?

Dear God,
Today I woke up. I'm healthy. I'm alive. I'm blessed. I apologize for all my complaining. I'm truly grateful for all you've done in my life. Amen.

AUTHOR UNKNOWN

OCTOBER 20, 2020

    I am having a bad Lupus flare today, so I have cancelled everything and decided to rest instead. I know that I cannot be helpful to anyone if I am exhausted and flaring. This flare is giving me a reminder to rest. I have found that this is God's way of saying "slow down". I hope everyone has a beautiful day and remembers to practice self care. Sending everyone love and light.

"Rest and self-care are so important. When you take time to replenish your spirit, it allows you to serve others from the overflow. You cannot serve from an empty vessel."

ELEANOR BROWNN

NOVEMBER 3, 2020

Hi everyone! I am so excited. I have almost completed my End of Life Doula training and will be certified soon by Lifespan Doulas. I have found myself thinking about my own death as I have been working on the various parts of this training. I am not afraid to die and I have wondered what scares people about death. God had recently given me an eye-opener through a dream I had the other night. I dreamt I was dying, and as I drew my last breath, I became afraid because I had to let go of all control and surrender to God. I believe this is one of the biggest fears most of us have: to truly let go of the control we think we have. I am grateful for this vision so I can be more empathetic towards my clients and prepare for my own death.

"The moment we take our last breath on earth, we take our first in heaven."

BILLY GRAHAM

MANY THANKS

"Gratitude is the wine for the soul. Go on. Get drunk." - Rumi

I want to get drunk now by telling the people in my life how thankful and grateful I am for their help and support. I feel strongly that I would have never written this book or strived to become an End of Life Doula and Reiki practitioner without them.

I want to thank God for all of the gifts He has given me in order to live my life to the fullest, despite my illnesses and struggles. Without my faith in God, I am not sure I would still be here in the physical world.

I want to thank my wonderful husband, John who has supported me in chasing my dreams. I am grateful to him for helping me through all my ups and downs on this crazy journey of chronic illness. He is a beautiful soul and my rock. I am also so grateful to my amazing son, Michael. He is such an old and beautiful soul who has supported me through my illnesses. He has acted with such courage and love even when I am in horrible pain or have been close to death. They both love me unconditionally even when I am at my lowest.

I want to thank Matt Buonocore and Alaina DaRin. They are my editors and dearest friends. They are the ones who felt I had a story to tell in the first place. They are both beautiful poets and gifted writers who have helped and encouraged me to write this book. They have put in a lot of hard work into this book. I will be forever grateful.

I want to thank all my family and friends that are

a part of my life. I am so blessed to have such a beautiful group of people in my life that support and care for me so deeply.

I want to thank Dr. Newton, nurse practitioner Allison, and the staff for saving my life. They are an amazing team in gastroenterology at Southwest Hospital, and I am forever grateful.

I want to thank Dr. Michael Cline at the Cleveland Clinic who helped me get off of tube feedings and to eat real food. Due to his research into my rare autoimmune disease, he was able to treat me so I could eat again. I am truly grateful and blessed.

I want to express deep gratitude to the nurses and staff at Seidman Cancer Center and St. Johns Westshore who helped me with all my various infusions. These hard workers are so compassionate and such wonderful souls.

I want to express my gratitude and thank my nurse, Karen from Acreedo who does my IVIG infusions every other week. She is a wonderful nurse and has helped and supported me through these tough times.

I want to thank my nurse, Sharon from Coram who does my Rituxan infusions twice every December and twice in June for my CNS Lupus. She is a beautiful soul whom I really appreciate.

Finally, I want to thank Keanu Reeves. As I mentioned before, he is also a warrior who keeps going in such a positive way. He is definitely a beautiful soul who shines his light to so many. I am truly grateful to him, his movies, and his interviews that help me stay so strong and positive.

CONTACT LAURA

Laura's business page: reiki-arete.com
Laura's business email: laura@reiki-arete.com
Laura's Facebook page,
Reiki-arete: https://www.facebook.com/biernack/